CONTENTS

WHERE IS BUCKINGHAM PALACE?

Buckingham Palace is
in the centre of London.
This very important
building is where
The Queen lives and
works during the week.
You can tell if The Queen
is in the Palace by looking
at the large flag flying
above the roof. If
The Queen is in the
Palace, the flag you'll
see will be the Royal
Standard. At the weekend,
The Queen travels to
Windsor Castle.

*The Union flag, often known
as the Union Jack, is flown
when The Queen is away.*

4

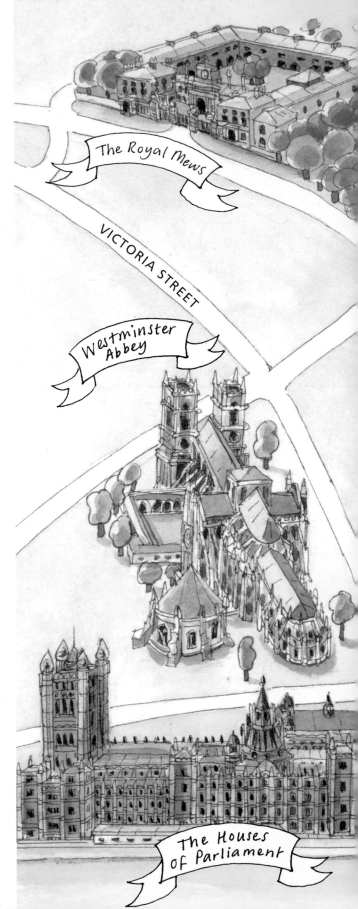

The Royal Mews

VICTORIA STREET

Westminster Abbey

The Houses of Parliament

5

The Guardsmen learn how to march, salute and stand still during hours and hours of drill practice.

GUARDING THE PALACE

Buckingham Palace is protected by Guardsmen. There is a famous ceremony called 'Changing of the Guard'. The Captain of the Guard hands over the key to the Palace to the New Guard. This happens when the New Guard march through the Palace gate. Then the Old Guard march back to their barracks.

This Guardsman from the Grenadier Guards is wearing a bearskin cap with a white feather and a bright red tunic with shiny brass buttons.

A ROYAL OFFICE
AND A HOME

Buckingham Palace has been a home to five queens, four kings, sixteen princes and twelve princesses. The present Queen is married to The Duke of Edinburgh and the Palace has been their home for more than 50 years. In the Palace, The Queen carries out her important job of meeting the British Prime Minister and leaders of other countries.

The Queen spends part of her morning reading letters. On her birthday, she receives thousands of birthday cards!

This is a portrait of The Queen's grandfather, King George V, who lived in Buckingham Palace.

Look, I can see a crown. In the painting – on the red cushion.

There are 650 rooms in the Palace, including lots of bedrooms and bathrooms. The State Rooms are the best rooms in the Palace. The Queen meets her most important guests in these rooms. They are full of amazing art gathered together by kings and queens. There are paintings, sculptures, vases, clocks – and sofas long enough for ten people to sit on.

In this painting, the present Queen's great-great-grandmother Queen Victoria is surrounded by five of her nine children.

11

A ROYAL BUILDING

There are crowns all over the inside and outside of Buckingham Palace – on doors, lamps, ceilings, and on picture frames. There is a crown and the letters 'EIIR' on The Queen's throne. The 'E' stands for Elizabeth and the 'R' stands for Regina, which means 'Queen' in Latin. The roman numeral 'II' means 'second'. This shows that the present Queen is the second queen to be called Elizabeth.

Whenever you see 'EIIR' on a letterbox, it means that it was made during the present Queen's reign.

The Queen's throne is the one with 'EIIR'. The Queen doesn't sit on her throne all day! She carries out royal duties all over the country.

Children are given badges and medals too.

I'm practising my curtsey.

MEETING THE QUEEN

If you meet The Queen, you begin by calling her 'Your Majesty' and then use 'Ma'am' for the rest of the conversation. Men and boys bow their heads and women and girls make a small curtsey. One of The Queen's most important jobs in Buckingham Palace is to give medals and honours to adults and children who've done something very special.

'Ma'am' is spoken to rhyme with 'jam'.

15

WEARING A CROWN

The Queen wears a crown on very important occasions. She wears the Imperial State Crown during the State Opening of Parliament, which happens every year. The Imperial State Crown has 2,868 diamonds, 273 pearls, 17 sapphires, 11 emeralds and 5 rubies. All of The Queen's crowns are kept safe in the Tower of London.

On the day of her Coronation in 1953, The Queen waves from the balcony of Buckingham Palace while wearing the Imperial State Crown.

Each year, 36,000 cups of tea, 45,000 sandwiches and 20,000 slices of cake and pastries are eaten in the Palace garden.

Mmmmm, this cake is delicious!

The Queen has a helicopter to help her travel around the country. Sometimes, it lands on the Palace garden lawn.

Every year, The Queen invites 24,000 people to her summer Garden Parties. Invitations are given to thank people for working hard. Guests drink tea, eat cakes, listen to music played by a band and, if they are very lucky, meet The Queen. In 2006, children were invited to the Palace for a special Garden Party with a picnic tea to celebrate The Queen's 80th birthday.

ROYAL ANIMALS

The Queen's favourite dogs are corgis. The Queen's corgis are called Linnet, Monty, Willow and Holly, and the dorgis, which are a mix of a corgi and a dachshund, are called Cider, Candy and Vulcan. The Queen's dogs travel with her in cars, on trains and on airplanes, unless she is travelling abroad.

Here, The Queen is riding her horse Tinkerbell. Her daughter Princess Anne is riding Peter Pan and her granddaughter Zara Phillips is riding Tiger Lily.

When The Queen is very busy, footmen take the dogs for their walks.

The royal chefs are always very busy making food for The Queen's staff and guests.

UPSTAIRS, DOWNSTAIRS

Housekeepers, chefs, florists, clockmakers, postmen, chauffeurs, gardeners and dressmakers all work at Buckingham Palace. There are royal kitchens, where food is made, royal cellars, where wine is stored, a flower room, where flowers are arranged, and a laundry, where clothes and tablecloths are cleaned and ironed.

Here is a footman polishing some of The Queen's silver. On another day, he might serve at a banquet.

23

BREAKFASTS TO BANQUETS

Royal chefs prepare food for breakfasts, lunches, dinners and State Banquets. A State Banquet is the busiest time for the royal kitchen. The chefs prepare four courses of food for up to 166 guests. It takes two days to lay the table for a State Banquet. More than 2,000 pieces of cutlery are used during the meal.

This looks like a real crown on a cushion. It's not! It is a cake baked by the royal chefs as a prize for children.

This is the biggest table I've ever seen.

Prince William and Catherine Middleton are now called The Duke and Duchess of Cambridge. Here they are walking into Buckingham Palace through the Grand Entrance.

The wedding dress is so beautiful!

ROYAL WEDDINGS

Many members of the Royal Family have been married in London. In 1947 The Queen and The Duke of Edinburgh were married in Westminster Abbey. In 2011, guests from around the world were invited to a wedding reception at Buckingham Palace to celebrate the marriage of The Queen's grandson Prince William to Catherine Middleton.

For his wedding cake, Prince William asked for a chocolate biscuit cake, which was made from a secret Royal Family recipe.

TRAVELLING IN STYLE

Although The Queen doesn't have a passport, she has travelled all over the world in horse-drawn carriages, cars, trains, helicopters and airplanes. Travelling by carriage is the best way for The Queen to be seen by the crowds. The Royal Train has bedrooms, bathrooms and a kitchen, so that The Queen and her family can travel overnight.

The Irish State Coach is often used by The Queen to travel to the State Opening of Parliament. It was built in Ireland over 200 years ago.

The Gold State Coach is covered in gold and has a crown on its roof.

29

There are always lots of parties to celebrate a Royal Jubilee.
There are so many people in front of the Palace!

THE BIGGEST CELEBRATION

When a king or queen reigns for a very long time, the whole country celebrates with a Royal Jubilee. A Silver Jubilee celebrates a reign of 25 years and a Golden Jubilee celebrates a reign of 50 years. The Queen celebrates 60 years of her reign with a Diamond Jubilee in 2012. Everyone is given a special holiday so they can celebrate too.

The Diamond Diadem is a small crown. It has 1,333 diamonds. The Queen is often seen wearing the Diamond Diadem on stamps and coins.

Look at **www.royalcollection.org.uk**
for information about visiting Buckingham Palace,
Windsor Castle and the Palace of Holyroodhouse

Written by Marion McAuley.
Published by Royal Collection Trust /
© HM Queen Elizabeth II 2011.
Reprinted 2011. This edition reprinted 2012.

Text and reproduction of all items in the Royal Collection
© 2011 HM Queen Elizabeth II.

013762

ISBN 978 1 905686 41 4

British Library Cataloguing in Publication Data: A catalogue
record for this book is available from the British Library.

Editorial Consultant: Susie Behar
Designer: Emily Wilkinson
Production Management: Debbie Wayment
Printed on 170 gsm Greencoat Silk
Printed and bound by Swallowtail Print

PICTURE CREDITS

All works reproduced are in the Royal Collection
unless indicated below. The Royal Collection
is grateful for permission to reproduce the following:

p. 4, Altrendo Travel/Getty Images
p. 6, © Pawel Libera/Corbis
p. 7, © Squared Studios/Getty Images
p. 8, 14, 16, 18, 29, 30, PA Photos
p. 9, photographer: Peter Smith
pp. 10, 13, photographer: Derry Moore
p. 17, photographer: Ian Jones
p. 19, Copyright reserved
p. 21, photographer: Christopher Simon Sykes
p. 22, photographer: Simon Roberson
p. 24, photographer: Mark Flanagan
p. 25, photographer: Simon Roberson
p. 26, photographer: Ian Jones
p. 27, PA Photos/© Clarence House
p. 28, photographer: David Cripps

Every effort has been made to contact
copyright holders; any omissions
are inadvertent and will be corrected
in future editions if notification
of the amended credit is sent
to the publisher in writing.

ACKNOWLEDGEMENTS

The permission of Her Majesty The Queen to reproduce
items from the Royal Collection is gratefully acknowledged.

In the preparation of this book I am indebted to many colleagues
for their assistance, including Dominic Brown, Nina Chang,
Zaki Cooper, Mark Flanagan, Edward Griffiths, Jacky Colliss
Harvey, Katie Holyoak, Kathryn Jones, Mark Lane, Karen Lawson,
Kate Owen, Daniel Partridge, Christopher Pittaway, Debbie
Wayment and Eva Zielinska-Millar.

I should like to thank the teachers and pupils of Montem Primary
School, St. Bernard's Preparatory School, Barrow Hill Junior School
and Abbeyhill Primary School for their valuable comments during
the development of this book.

I hope you've had a wonderful time visiting the Palace. How many crowns did you find?

FSC
www.fsc.org
MIX
Paper from
responsible sources
FSC® C023146

WORLD
LAND
TRUST™
www.carbonbalancedpaper.com
CBP0006440706113012

There are 36 crowns inside this book!